Career Exploration

Careers If You Like to Travel

Peggy J. Parks

ReferencePoint
Press®

San Diego, CA

About the Author

Peggy J. Parks loves being an author and has written dozens of educational books on a wide variety of topics for teens and young adults. She holds a bachelor's degree from Aquinas College in Grand Rapids, Michigan, where she graduated magna cum laude. Parks lives in Muskegon, Michigan, a town she says inspires her writing because of its location on the shores of beautiful Lake Michigan.

For more information, contact:
ReferencePoint Press, Inc.
PO Box 27779
San Diego, CA 92198
www.ReferencePointPress.com

Picture Credits:

Cover: Digital Vision/iStockphoto.com
24: J.W. Walker/Newscom
33: gorodenkoff/iStockphoto.com
40: Monkey Business Images/Shutterstock.com
48: Gabriele Maricchiolo/Zuma Press/Newscom
59: iStockphoto.com

LIBRARY OF CONGRESS CATALOGING-IN-PUBLICATION DATA

Name: Parks, Peggy J., 1951– author.
Title: Careers If You Like to Travel/by Peggy J. Parks.
Description: San Diego, CA: ReferencePoint Press, Inc., 2020. | Series:
  Career Exploration | Includes bibliographical references and index. |
  Audience: Grade 9 to 12.
Identifiers: LCCN 2018051673 (print) | LCCN 2018057688 (ebook) | ISBN
  9781682825983 (eBook) | ISBN 9781682825976 (hardback)
Subjects: LCSH: Tourism—Vocational guidance—Juvenile literature.
Classification: LCC G155.5 (ebook) | LCC G155.5 .P37 2020 (print) | DDC
  910.23—dc23
LC record available at https://lccn.loc.gov/2018051673

Contents

Careers on the Move

The teenage years can be a crazy whirlwind of activity. Days are so packed with classes, homework, studying, sports, extracurricular activities, and family obligations that it can seem like there isn't enough time to fit everything in. With all this and more going on, the idea of planning for a career that is still years down the road may be very low on the priority list. But thinking about the future and what you might want to do for a living is important because the high school years can fly by. It is much better to do some early career planning than to find yourself at high school graduation without any clue what you're going to do next.

A Good Starting Point

Career planning does not mean that you need to decide on a career while you're a teenager. In fact, most young people change their minds over and over again before settling on a definite career choice. Think of planning as the beginning of a journey toward discovery—a process that can help you think about the future and start shaping it. "My feeling is that high school students don't have to know the exact career they want," says career counselor Mark Danaher, "but they should know how to explore careers and put time into investigating them and learning about their skills and interests."[1]

Career counselors agree that evaluating one's personal skills and interests is a good way to start the career planning process. Although many young people have no idea what they want to do with their lives, they probably have a very good idea of what types of activities they enjoy and what interests them. By focusing on these interests, they could be laying the foundation for a fulfilling, enjoyable career. "Where do your interests lie?" asks counselor Jacqueline Dautaj. "Are you fascinated by how things work? Maybe you love the written word. Zeroing in on your interests will help steer you in the right direction for a career, and choosing a path you're already interested in will keep you happier in the long run."[2]

Once someone's interests have been identified, the next step is researching careers that could put those interests to use. (A high school guidance counselor can help with this.) Teens who enjoy working with kids, for example, might consider a career as a child care worker, teacher, or school counselor. Those who enjoy taking gadgets apart and putting them back together again might look into engineering, computer science, or some other kind of technical field. Someone with a passion for helping others, like Hannah Kardohely, may want to explore nursing, social work, or other careers in health care. Kardohely graduated from high school in June 2018. When she was in middle school, an experience with her mother piqued her interest in a possible physical therapy career. "I used to give my mom shoulder massages," she says, "and I thought it would be cool to figure out how to fix the rest of the body."[3]

More than Just a Dream

Planning a career based on what they like to do can benefit teens with a wide range of interests, including those who love to travel. Perhaps you are one of them: someone who dreams of having a job that allows you to be on the move, traveling to distant places and, in the process, earning a good living. If so, this could be more than merely a dream because such careers really do exist.

Dozens of careers involve travel, not only domestically but also worldwide. Some of these are well known, such as flight attendant, travel agent, cruise ship employee, or tour guide. But many other exciting, enjoyable careers also involve travel, such as hospitality managers, who work at major hotels and resorts all over the world. "There are hotels everywhere," says Melissa Williams, who works as a human resources manager at the Hilton Lisle Hotel in Naperville, Illinois. "You can go anywhere in the world . . . well, maybe not Antarctica! . . . but you'll have an opportunity for a career in hospitality."[4] Other careers that involve travel include event planner, humanitarian aid worker, English as a second language (ESL) teacher, travel nurse, athletic scout, and various jobs in Foreign Service for the US Department of State. These are only a few of the numerous opportunities available to people who want to combine earning a living with their love of travel.

Go for It!

For students in high school, or even middle school, who are starting to think about the future, career planning needn't be a stressful or intimidating task. Start by focusing on what you like to do most and what you want to spend as much time as possible doing. If you dream about a career that involves traveling to exotic places, don't give up on that dream. Instead, figure out how to make it happen. "If the travel bug has bitten you, stop ignoring it," says career coach Ashley Stahl. "Stop telling yourself that a job you love that sends you around the world is outside the realm of possibilities—it's not!"[5]

Hospitality Manager

What Does a Hospitality Manager Do?

The word *hospitality* refers to providing friendly service, housing, and entertainment to guests—and that is precisely what hospitality management is all about. *Hospitality manager* is an umbrella term that refers to management professionals who oversee service establishments. For those who dream of traveling, a hospitality management career could be ideal because the job could take them most anywhere in the world. Hospitality managers are in charge of posh resorts in the Caribbean; five-star hotels in London, Paris, and Rome; bed-and-breakfasts in New England's small, picturesque villages; casinos in Las Vegas, Nevada, or Monaco's famed Monte Carlo; and the luxury accommodations of cruise ships.

Hospitality management professionals' titles vary widely from job to job. They may be called general manager, operations manager, lodging manager, director, or chief executive, just to name a few. As different as their jobs and titles may be, the one responsibility these professionals share is ensuring that guests receive the best service possible during a visit.

Since they are ultimately accountable for every aspect of their facility's operations, hospitality managers have a tremendous amount of responsibility. They oversee not only public areas such as reception, lobbies, restaurants, and concierge services but also departments that are behind the scenes, including maintenance, housekeeping, kitchens, sales and marketing, security, catering services, and valet parking, among others. Although day-to-day oversight is typically handled by departmental supervisors, hospitality managers are still ultimately responsible.

A hospitality manager's duties can vary a great deal, according to the size and location of the establishment and how many guests it can accommodate. Some common duties include ensuring that appropriate standards for guest services, decor, and housekeeping are met; tracking how much money the facility is making on a daily, weekly, and monthly basis; inspecting guest rooms, public areas, and grounds for cleanliness and appearance; recruiting, interviewing, hiring, and sometimes firing staff members; setting room rates and budgets, approving expenditures, and allocating funds to individual departments; and being available for problems that need to be resolved—in some cases twenty-four hours a day.

Along with their focus on guests, hospitality managers must also work hard to maintain excellent relationships with their staff, creating an environment in which employees feel valued. "I have to make sure my staff is happy because they are just as important as the guests," says an operations manager from a major hotel in Louisiana. "If you check in to a hotel with an unhappy staff, it shows. So I have to make sure everyone communicates any problems or opinions; that includes daily meetings with the managers of every department."[6]

The Workday

Because of the nature of the hospitality industry, top managers of hotels and resorts agree that there is no such thing as a typical day. They must contend with an ever-changing environment and always expect the unexpected, being prepared to handle problems and emergencies quickly and efficiently. "No day will be the same," says

The Special Touch

"In today's world people want a memorable, human experience. The most enjoyable for a client is to receive a product or service that no one else could experience—to make them feel unique. Once we had a guest staying with us who cried when he discovered a frame with his favourite Instagram picture in his room. He had taken it in New Zealand and told one of our team members how memorable was his stay there. We always try to exceed the expectations and surprise guests—to make their stay unique and memorable."

—Katja Henke, general manager of the Peninsula Paris Hotel in Paris, France

Quoted in Franck Demaury, "Meeting with Katja Henke, General Manager at Peninsula Paris," Luxury Design, October 5, 2016. www.luxury-design.com.

Rachel Banks, learning and development manager at the Savoy Hotel in London, "as there is always great diversity in the work you carry out, the people you work with and the guests that you meet."[7]

One aspect of their job that hospitality managers share is that their days are jam packed. "It's always busy,"[8] says Rommel Gopez, the director of guest relations at New York City's historic Hotel Edison. Each morning, Gopez arrives at the hotel around 6:30 a.m., and the first thing he does is check his schedule for the day. He reviews the facility's arrivals and occupancy and looks to see how many VIPs are staying. He checks his email, creates reports (such as who the VIPs are and what has to be done for them), and attends meetings. Throughout the day most of Gopez's time revolves around guests and employees, as he explains: "I'm in the lobby talking to guests, showing rooms to guests, talking to my team about what's coming up and any other issues."[9] Gopez says that his day typically ends around 5:00 or 6:00 p.m.

Gopez is passionate about the hospitality business. There are many reasons for this, such as having the privilege of getting to know interesting people from all over the world. That goes along with his fondness for traveling, as he explains: "I'll talk to someone from one country and then think, 'Oh, I should travel there next.' And when I do travel there, I already have a friend."[10]

It All Started with Ice Cream

"My parents used to have an ice cream shop in Munich, and this is where it all started. I would come home after school and clean the dishes or make ice cream. . . . Then at 16 I got an internship with Hilton International. . . . I always focused on food and beverage—my dream was to become a maître d—and then when I was a restaurant manager my dream was to become a director of food and beverage. . . . I think once I exhausted that journey in hotels, it was about how much more creativity and input I could give."

—Christian Zandonella, general manager of the Ritz-Carlton in Vienna, Austria

Quoted in Steven Bond, "Interview: Christian Zandonella, General Manager of the Ritz-Carlton, Vienna," Destination of the World News, September 6, 2017. www.dotwnews.com.

Education and Training

Many hospitality managers have bachelor's degrees in hotel or hospitality management, culinary management, marketing, business, or another discipline. Earning a college degree can give aspiring hospitality managers an edge over those with lesser degrees or those who did not attend college. Yet in the hospitality industry, on-the-job experience is sometimes valued as much as or even more than a college education. Many hospitality managers started out in lower-level positions and then worked their way up the ladder. Through this experience, they developed a keen understanding of the various hotel jobs by experiencing them firsthand.

This was the case with Ben Booker, who is now general manager of Ashdown Park Hotel & Country Club in East Sussex, United Kingdom. After leaving high school, Booker worked in jobs at several different hotels in the United Kingdom. He held positions in housekeeping and room service and eventually became a doorman. Over the following years he worked his way up to food and beverage manager at one hotel and then accepted a position of deputy manager at a different hotel. In 2007 he became the general manager at Ashdown Park. "Through hard work and passion," says Booker, "I have worked my way up to manage a four-star, luxury hotel."[11]

Skills and Personality

Some people are cut out to work in the hospitality field, and some are not. "When I first began my journey into the hospitality world," says Melissa Williams, human resources manager at the Hilton Lisle Hotel in Naperville, Illinois, "one of my mentors told me 'there is no middle ground in hospitality, you will either love it, or hate it.' After more than ten years in the industry, I agree 100%."[12] One of the most important traits for hospitality managers is being superb communicators, including the ability to listen well and express themselves clearly. They need excellent leadership and problem-solving skills, a positive attitude, and a firm commitment to customer service. And they must love being around people because hospitality management is by no means a solitary profession.

Also essential for hospitality managers is the ability to remain calm and professional even in the midst of chaos. They never know what sorts of problems might develop, and they must keep their cool no matter what happens. A Louisiana hotel manager shares his experience: "Countless times I've had guests up in my face screaming and even occasionally threatening violence because of something somebody else did or something totally out of my control, but I stayed cool and just listened to them, let them know that I was listening, and eventually they calmed down too."[13]

Working Conditions

Hospitality management is typically an indoor job, although those in charge of sprawling resorts may spend quite a bit of time walking the grounds. Hospitality managers spend time in their offices and in conference rooms where they meet with their staff. They also wander around their facilities, conducting inspections, visiting with customers, and resolving problems.

The hours a hospitality manager works can be wildly unpredictable. Even if a manager is scheduled for the daytime shift, most hotels and resorts never close, and crises involving customers or employees may require attention at any time of the day or night. "The worst part of my job is that it's a 24 hour-a-day, 365 day-a-year business," says the Louisiana hotel manager. "It does get tiring. Sometimes I just wish that we could lock the front door and unplug the phones for two days. You sacrifice time with your friends and family and/or you burn out and start to develop bad habits to cope, unless you're careful."[14]

Employers and Pay

Hospitality managers are employed by hotels and resorts all over the world. The money they earn depends on a number of factors, such as the size, class, and geographic location of the facility. Larger establishments located in major cities pay more, often a lot more, than smaller hotels and resorts. Other factors affecting salary include years of experience in the hospitality industry and a manager's individual work performance.

The Bureau of Labor Statistics (BLS), referring to lodging managers, says the annual salary ranges from a low of $28,930 to more than $98,370. According to the online compensation resource Salary.com, the range is considerably wider, with hotel managers earning from $72,976 to $133,847. A number of positions posted on the job search website Glassdoor offer general managers of major hotels and resorts up to $165,000 per year.

What Is the Future Job Outlook for Hospitality Managers?

According to the BLS, lodging managers held 47,800 jobs in 2016. This is projected to grow 4 percent through 2026, which represents about nineteen hundred new jobs. Industry predictions show even higher growth in the coming years. According to a March 2018 article in the *Wall Street Journal*, hospitality is one of the fastest-growing industries, with 5 to 6 percent growth as of 2018. This growth is expected to continue—which means employment opportunities for aspiring hospitality managers and lower-level positions that can eventually work up to that. Gopez is witnessing that for himself. "We have hotels popping up left and right in New York City," he says. "A lot of great hotels are popping up in Brooklyn these days. That's a lot of positions that need to be filled."[15]

Find Out More

American Hotel & Lodging Educational Institute (AHLEI)
6751 Forum Dr., Suite 220
Orlando, FL 32821
website: www.ahlei.org

The AHLEI provides hospitality education, training, and professional certification for people who seek careers in the hospitality industry. Its blog offers a collection of articles on topics of interest to those who are interested in hospitality careers, including students who are starting to think about their career.

Capterra Blogs
website: https://blog.capterra.com

Capterra is a software review platform, but its blog offers numerous articles about careers, including in the hospitality field. The site search engine produces articles on education for aspiring hospitality managers, who is best suited for a career in hospitality, steps to getting a job in hospitality, and many other related topics.

HCareers
website: www.hcareers.com

HCareers is an online resource for the hospitality industry, including employers, current hospitality employees, and job seekers. The website is a valuable resource for those audiences, with a search engine that produces a variety of hospitality-related articles, as well as a special career section with its own search engine.

International Hotel & Restaurant Association (IHRA)
5 Avenue Theodore Flournoy
1207 Geneva, Switzerland
website: www.ih-ra.org

The IHRA, which refers to itself as the voice of the hospitality industry, represents the interests of the hotel and restaurant industries worldwide. Its website features a variety of publications that may be of interest to those who are interested in a hospitality career.

Event Planner

A Few Facts

Number of Jobs
About 116,700 in 2016

Pay
About $26,390 to
$83,000

**Educational
Requirements**
Bachelor's degree usually
required

Personal Qualities
Outgoing personality,
good communication
and interpersonal skills,
organizational and
project-management
skills, ability to negotiate,
problem-solving expertise

Work Settings
In offices and at event
sites in a wide variety of
locations

Future Job Outlook
Projected 11 percent
growth rate through
2026

What Does an Event Planner Do?

The field of event planning involves envisioning, planning, and supervising all kinds of special events. These events may include conventions and trade shows, formal galas, themed parties for special occasions, sales meetings, weddings from small and simple to glitzy and star studded, fund-raisers for charities, sporting events, rock concerts, and everything in between. The Austin, Texas, event-planning company Kennedy says on its website:

> "Event planning" is an all-encompassing term that conjures a lot of different images for different people. Some hear the term "event planner" and immediately think "weddings," while others picture elaborate corporate conferences with ice sculptures, fire dancers and canapés for days. . . . The answer to the question, "What kinds of events do event planners produce?" is, honestly, "*All* the kinds."[16]

Along with "event planner," these professionals may be called event managers, event directors, or a variety of other titles.

An event planner's specific duties can vary a great deal, but some tasks are common to all who work in this profession. When organizing an event, the first step is meeting with clients to discuss the purpose, such as celebrating a company's fiftieth anniversary or pulling potential donors together to support a charity. Then the actual planning starts, with details such as theme, time, location, and budget being worked out and reviewed with the client. Planners solicit bids from event venues and service providers and visit venues to inspect them and ensure they meet the client's needs. They coordinate all services that will be needed for the event, including banquet rooms and seating, food, entertainment, and transportation.

On the day of the event, planners are in charge of ensuring that everything goes as planned and addressing any problems that develop. After the event is over, planners oversee teardown and cleanup of the venue, review invoices from vendors, and issue payments according to the client's approved budget. Once all the details are wrapped up, planners often dive into the next event and start the process all over again.

The Workday

Event planners juggle a wide variety of duties, which means that each day is different and the word *typical* doesn't necessarily apply. One thing they all have in common is how packed their schedules are. Alexis Roumeliotis, an event manager for the New York City–based career group known as the Muse, likes being busy and also likes that her job keeps her moving. "I can't sit at my desk for more than 30 minutes,"[17] she says.

Roumeliotis is usually up at 6:00 a.m. and ready to start her day. If there is a morning event, she arrives at the site about an hour before it starts in order to get things set up. "I assemble gift bags, arrange the chairs, do the flower arrangements, and prep the food and tech,"[18] she says. She also checks her email to see whether extra guests have been added to the attendee list and determine whether she needs to add chairs or tables or order additional items. When the event starts, typically around 8:00 or

9:00 a.m., Roumeliotis works the room, introducing people, making sure everyone has a name tag, and fetching refreshments and beverages as needed. Immediately after the event is over, she thanks guests for attending, chats with clients to get their feedback and discuss future events, and assists with cleanup.

Back in her office, Roumeliotis spends the afternoon on a variety of tasks. She catches up on emails, attends sales meetings, and takes care of details for other events she is working on. Later in the afternoon she meets with the marketing team to discuss goals and upcoming events. "I like to walk them through the plan and schedule,"[19] she says. She spends some more time writing and answering emails, makes her to-do list for the following day, and is usually out of the office by about 6:00 p.m.

Education, Training, and Certification

Most people who work as event planners have earned a bachelor's degree. Common fields of study include marketing, business management, public relations, and communications. Typically, event planners move into their jobs after spending several years in event assistant or event coordinator positions, which have given them the experience they need to take charge of events. Another way aspiring event planners can gather experience is by doing volunteer work for nonprofit organizations or charities.

Events director Elizabeth Conway, who owns the New York City firm Conway Amling Strategies and Events, says that volunteering can provide aspiring event planners with invaluable experience. "Working an event, whether it's sitting at the check-in table, procuring silent auction items, or helping spread the word to get attendees, is all easy experience to get if you're willing to work for it," she explains. "And an added bonus is that you're helping to do some good at the same time."[20]

Many seasoned event planners earn professional certification, and they highly recommend it for aspiring planners. "You want to be taken more seriously and make more money as an event professional? Get your certification,"[21] says Lindsay Martin-Bilbrey, a strategic events and marketing executive from Dallas, Texas. Martin-Bilbrey earned her Certified Meeting Professional (CMP) certification from the Events Industry Council. The most widely recognized certification for event planners, the CMP requires a minimum of thirty-six months of event-management experience, recent employment in an event-management job, and proof of continuing education credits. Those who have met these criteria must pass an exam that covers a variety of topics, from strategic planning and finance to logistics.

Skills and Personality

An outgoing, friendly personality is crucial for event planners because their jobs require near-constant interaction with people. For that same reason, they need excellent communication and interpersonal skills, as well as project-management skills, the ability to negotiate, creative thinking, and keen problem-solving expertise. The ability to multitask is also essential, because event planners have to juggle priorities and a multitude of details on a daily basis.

Another necessary trait for event planners is the ability to remain calm in stressful situations. Even after weeks or months of meticulous planning, events do not always go according to plan. In fact, there are times when an event quickly changes into a crisis situation. Mike Shea, who organizes and directs South by Southwest (SXSW), a massive annual conference and festival in

Austin, Texas, has experienced a number of unfortunate events, one of which he remembers vividly. "One year, massive downpours turned a grassy park into muck and mire, threatening two days of free concerts," says Shea. He kept his wits about him and, using some creative thinking, came up with a solution: blanketing the muddy park with hay. "We paced the park from end to end and arbitrarily determined that 10 steps equaled one bale of hay,"[22] says Shea. After the festival was over, the muddy hay needed to be removed from the park. Shea hired a group of men who used pitchforks to remove it and haul it away.

Working Conditions

Event planners tend to move around a lot; in other words, this is not the job for someone who prefers to work at a desk in an office all day. From attending meetings with clients and vendors to visiting and inspecting potential event venues to running countless errands to help an event come together, the schedules kept by event planners can seem impossible at times. "Long hours, weekends at work, and hardly any sleep are usually the formula event planners see when slaving away at all of the little details," says event-management consultant Holly Barker. "Be sure you're up for a big challenge if you decide to join the circus of event planning!"[23]

One of the top benefits of the job for event planners who love to travel is visiting the locations where the events are being held. That may involve travel to cities throughout the United States or to locations anywhere in the world. "From small towns to exotic resort destinations, traveling as an event planner can have some great perks!" says Barker. "While hard at work months or even years leading up to an event, you get to see it all come together in some very cool locations!"[24]

Employers and Pay

According to the Bureau of Labor Statistics (BLS), event planners (including meeting and convention planners) held about 116,700 jobs in 2016. The largest of these employers were religious, grantmaking, civic, and professional organizations; accommodation and food services; arts, entertainment, and recreation; administrative and support services; and self-employed event planners.

The money earned by event planners can vary a great deal, as it is based on factors such as years of experience, size of client (large clients have the largest budgets), the type of event, and how long the planning takes. The BLS reports that event planner salaries ranged from $26,390 to more than $82,980 per year as of May 2017. Research has shown that event planner salaries are commensurate with years of experience. A May 2017 survey by the Professional Convention Management Association, for example, found that the average annual salary for planners with one to three years of experience was $51,754; four to five years, $62,000; six to eight years, $69,976; nine to ten years, $74,155; and ten-plus years, $92,553.

What Is the Future Job Outlook for Event Planners?

The BLS projects a promising future for aspiring event planners. From 2016 to 2026, the projected job growth is 11 percent, which equates to 12,700 new jobs. "Demand for professionally planned meetings and events is expected to remain steady as businesses and organizations continue to host events regularly,"[25] says the BLS.

Find Out More

Event Manager Blog (EventMB)
website: www.eventmanagerblog.com

EventMB is an online resource for event professionals. It offers a large collection of industry reports and articles on topics such as qualities that event planners need, tips for planning events, how to start an event-planning business, and resources that can help aspiring event planners break into the industry.

Events Industry Council
2025 M St. NW, Suite 800
Washington, DC 20036
website: www.eventscouncil.org

The Events Industry Council, which represents firms and individuals involved in meeting and event planning, is the professional organization that awards the CMP certification. Its website offers news articles and a number of publications related to careers in the event-planning industry.

MeetingsNet
website: www.meetingsnet.com

MeetingsNet is an online resource packed with helpful information for professional event planners, as well as those who are interested in learning about being an event planner. The website's search engine produces numerous articles on a variety of topics related to the field of event planning.

National Association of Event Planners
website: www.nationalassociationofeventplanners.com

The National Association of Event Planners promotes high standards and integrity in the event-planning field by providing resources and education to event-planning professionals. Its website offers a variety of articles about the profession of event planning, as well as helpful information for those who aspire to become event planners.

Flight Attendant

A Few Facts

Number of Jobs
About 116,600 in 2016

Pay
About $26,860 to
$79,520 as of May 2017

**Educational
Requirements**
Minimum of high school
diploma; once hired,
extensive training at the
airline's flight-training
center

Personal Qualities
Good customer-service
and communication
skills, attentiveness,
physical stamina, good
decision-making skills,
ability to remain calm in
emergency situations

Work Settings
The cabin of an aircraft

Future Job Outlook
Projected 10 percent
growth rate through 2026

What Does a Flight Attendant Do?

Flight attendants are customer service professionals who perform their jobs thousands of feet in the air. They work crazy schedules, sometimes have to deal with drunk and disorderly passengers, and are away from home for long periods of time, but they get to travel—a lot. Flight attendants have a wide variety of responsibilities and duties. These may vary according to the airline, size of the aircraft, and duration of a flight, but the basic duties are the same. For instance, before a scheduled flight, the captain holds a preflight briefing for the entire crew. These briefings provide flight attendants with information such as how long the flight will last, the route the plane will be traveling, and expected weather conditions. Following the briefing, flight attendants conduct preflight inspections of emergency equipment to make sure all are working properly. They also inspect the cabin (where passengers are seated for the flight) to make sure it is clean, and they check to see that there is an ample supply of whatever food and beverages are needed for the flight.

When passengers are boarding, flight attendants greet them and provide any needed assistance. Once all passengers are on board and the aircraft is ready to depart, flight attendants ensure that passengers have their seat belts fastened and that tray tables are in the upright position. During the flight they serve beverages, snacks, and sometimes meals, and assist passengers as needed. Of all their duties, a flight attendant's primary responsibility is to ensure passenger safety. "People think we are just there to serve up Cokes and attitude," says a flight attendant named Riley, "but we're fully equipped to save you and your loved ones in an emergency." These emergencies may range from fighting a fire in the cabin to directing a passenger evacuation during an emergency landing.

After a midair disaster occurred in April 2018, flight attendants were praised for their handling of the emergency situation. A Southwest Airlines flight was en route from New York City to Dallas, Texas, when one of its engines suddenly exploded. The blast sprayed the aircraft with shards of metal, causing a window to shatter and the cabin to quickly lose air pressure. A female passenger was sucked into the shattered window. Flight attendants enlisted the help of other nearby passengers to pull her back and provide CPR. Sadly, she did not survive.

When the aircraft approached Philadelphia, Pennsylvania, for an emergency landing, flight attendants instructed passengers to put their heads down and brace themselves. The pilot successfully landed the crippled aircraft, and flight attendants directed passengers toward the aircraft door. Later, many of those passengers expressed their gratitude for how the flight attendants conducted themselves during a terrible situation. "Without a doubt in my mind, those individuals are heroes," says Kristopher Johnson, a passenger on the flight.

A Typical Workday

All flight attendants have a home base, which is the airport they fly out of and into. Their schedules are composed of blocks of time known as duty periods. In general, flight attendants work four

Her Dream Job

"My background is in customer service; I have worked in banking, fitness, and recruitment but never travel. I've always loved travelling and thought being a flight attendant would be a cool job, but I actually ended up at this job by fluke. I stumbled on an ad for a flight attendant job and applied, never thinking I would actually even get an interview. But I did and here I am, living the dream."

—Jennifer Greene, a flight attendant with the Canadian airline WestJet Encore

Quoted in Workopolis, "What's It Like Working as a Flight Attendant?," February 2018. https://careers.workopolis.com.

flights per day, which amounts to an average of twelve to fourteen hours per duty period. The Federal Aviation Administration mandates that they receive at least nine consecutive hours of rest following any duty period before starting their next duty period.

Some flight attendants (known as commuters) live in a different location from their base, so they must commute to work. This is the case with Robert Bingochea, a United Airlines flight attendant who commutes to Denver, Colorado, from his home in Phoenix, Arizona. Whenever Bingochea is scheduled to work, he flies to Denver the afternoon before and spends the night at a hotel so there is no danger of missing his scheduled flight. "You can't be late. . . . You have to be there on time," he says. Upon arrival at the Denver airport, he goes through security screening and then lets staff know he is there and ready to go. When it is time to board the aircraft, Bingochea stows his suitcase and gets ready for the pilot's preflight briefing.

Bingochea and his fellow flight attendants go to their assigned crew stations in the aircraft and do their preflight checks. This involves checking the galleys (tiny kitchens where food is prepared), bathrooms, and overhead bins. As passengers board, flight attendants greet them and offer assistance to those with special needs. Once the doors are closed and locked and the aircraft is rolled back from the gate, the captain alerts the crew to be seated

A flight attendant demonstrates safety measures in case of emergency. Whether on a domestic or international flight, the primary job of a flight attendant is to make sure passengers are safe and comfortable.

for departure. After the plane takes off and has reached cruising altitude, it is time for beverage service to begin. For Bingochea, this is when he has a chance to make his way through the aisles and talk with passengers. "You make a big difference when you interact with people," he says. "People will remember you, either by what you did or what you didn't do."

When the flight is over, the aircraft has landed, and all passengers have deplaned, Bingochea heads toward the gate for his next departure. There he repeats the process over again until he has completed his last assigned flight for the day. He then catches a standby flight back home to Phoenix. If all flights are full and he cannot get a seat, he spends the night in Denver and flies home the next day.

Education and Training

The minimum education needed to be accepted into an airline's training program is a high school diploma, although many airlines prefer applicants to have at least some college. Another preference is for applicants to have several years of experience working in some kind of service occupation, such as in a hotel, restaurant, or other business that serves the public.

Flight training programs last anywhere from three to eight weeks and are typically held at the airline's flight training center. Trainees must learn an incredible amount of information during their training, and it can be overwhelming. Jennifer Greene, who is a flight attendant with the Canadian regional airline WestJet Encore, says that training is a "grueling" experience, as she explains: "You cover it all, from putting out fires and giving first aid, to evacuating an entire plane in record time. There are regular tests and those who don't pass are cut immediately, so you really need to be prepared to work and study hard to get through."

Skills and Personality

Flight attendants constantly work with people, so they must have a pleasant personality and be able to communicate well. Other necessary skills include attentiveness, good decision-making, and physical stamina, because they work for hours on their feet and often must hurry from gate to gate when changing flights. Also, it is essential that flight attendants remain levelheaded when faced with stressful or emergency situations. "A good flight attendant has to have a little bit of everything," says Greene. "You need to be observant, a good communicator and leader, calm under fire, super organized and a stickler for following rules, but you also have to think fast on your feet, and be flexible and ready to roll with the punches—it's a very unique job."

Working Conditions

Aspiring flight attendants should be aware that the job is far from a typical nine-to-five career. According to the Bureau of Labor Statistics (BLS), flight attendants typically work on aircraft seventy-five to one hundred hours per month. They spend about fifty additional hours per month on the ground conducting tasks such as preparing flights, writing reports, and waiting for aircraft to arrive.

Depending on the airline and their assigned destinations, they may spend several nights each week (or even longer periods) away from home.

Flight attendants who are just starting out are usually on call, meaning they do not have a set schedule. Rather, they are called into work on demand and must be at the airport within two hours. Another challenge for new flight attendants is that they often end up working the holidays and weekends that their peers with more seniority don't want to work. "There will be missed birthdays, recitals, parties and games," says flight attendant Carrie A. Trey. She loves her job but urges aspiring flight attendants to "know what you're getting into." She writes:

> One of the most important things I recommend before you apply is to do some research and make sure you understand what the job is really like. . . . You will sometimes be working long days—or even all night—and it's not all going to be serving Champagne. . . . The job is by no means as fancy or glamorous as some people make it out to be. If that doesn't sound like something you'd be comfortable with, turn around now!

Employers and Pay

The largest employers of flight attendants in the United States are the major commercial airlines. These include Alaska Airlines, American Airlines, Delta Air Lines, Frontier Airlines, Hawaiian Airlines, JetBlue Airways, Southwest Airlines, Spirit Airlines, and United Airlines. Small, regional airlines also employ flight attendants, as do some major corporations that have their own corporate jets.

Flight attendants are paid hourly, per their flying time. Their salaries, according to the BLS, ranged from $26,860 per year to nearly $80,000 per year as of May 2017. The consumer career resource Salary.com publicizes a high salary range for flight attendants, from about $59,000 to more than $91,000.

Favorite Career Moment

"On an Atlanta to Orlando flight, a 6-year-old girl named Lindsay, in a wheelchair with Cerebral Palsy, was wheeled down the Jetway by her mom. . . . I offered to carry Lindsay to her seat and was taken up on my offer immediately. . . . She put her arms around my neck, and on the way to her seat I talked to her about what fun she would have [at Disney World]. When I carried her back to her wheelchair after landing in Orlando she didn't want to let go of my neck, and that gesture completely melted me. I'll never forget little Lindsay."

—Danny Elkins, a flight attendant with Delta Air Lines

Quoted in Rachel Gillett, "What It's Really Like to Be a Flight Attendant," Business Insider, November 17, 2017. www.businessinsider.com.

Along with being paid well, flight attendants enjoy many perks, and being able to travel is the most popular perk of all. "Yes, I fly for free," says a Delta Airlines flight attendant named Daphni Edwards. "Although it's something I've grown accustomed to, it's not something I could EVER take for granted. Free flights are definitely the best and most beautiful part of this job." During their time off, flight attendants can travel anywhere their airline flies. Their seats on a particular flight depend on availability, as Edwards explains: "Although the flights are free, our seats are not guaranteed. Everyone flies standby, and open seats on a flight go to people in order of seniority and priority."

What Is the Future Job Outlook for Flight Attendants?

In 2016 flight attendants in the United States held about 116,600 jobs. The need for these professionals is expected to grow 10 percent through 2026, with an estimated 11,900 new jobs being created. Aspiring flight attendants need to be aware, though, that the field is highly competitive, and there are far more applicants than available jobs. Delta Air Lines, for instance, advertised its intention to hire 1,200 flight attendants in 2016—and the airline received 150,000 applications.

Find Out More

Association of Flight Attendants (AFA)
501 Third St. NW
Washington, DC 20001
website: www.afacwa.org

Representing nearly fifty thousand flight attendants at twenty airlines, the AFA is the world's largest flight attendant labor union. Its website offers a valuable collection of publications of interest and concern to flight attendants and those who are interested in a flight attendant career.

Bureau of Labor Statistics (BLS)
Office of Occupational Statistics and Employment Projections
PSB Suite 2135, 2 Massachusetts Ave. NE
Washington, DC 20212
website: www.bls.gov

The BLS is the United States's chief statistical agency responsible for measuring labor market activity, working conditions, and economic price changes. Visitors to its website will find an informative publication called *Occupational Outlook Handbook: Flight Attendants*, which discusses duties, work environment, education and training, pay, and job outlook.

Flight Attendant Life
website: https://flightattendantlife.com/blog

Flight Attendant Life is a blog especially for those who work as flight attendants. It features hundreds of archived posts on a variety of topics, including problems experienced by flight attendants, tips for staying healthy, flight attendant training, common myths, the best airlines to work for, and flight attendant schedules.

The Points Guy: Carrie A. Trey
website: https://thepointsguy.com/author/cary-a-trey

Carrie A. Trey is the pseudonym for a flight attendant who writes prolifically about the industry and her career. Articles found on this website are archived and cover a wide variety of topics, such as how to become a flight attendant, issues with passengers, cabin crew challenges, travel tips, the flight attendant lifestyle, and much more.

Construction Engineer

What Does a Construction Engineer Do?

Construction engineering is a subset of civil engineering. Although the two share many similarities, there are distinct differences between them. Civil engineers, for example, focus more on the design, planning, and analysis of a construction project. Construction engineers are also involved in those activities, but they are typically the hands-on people. Most of their time is spent at job sites managing projects to ensure that they are constructed in accordance with plans and specifications and are completed on time and within the approved budget. Projects range from residential housing developments to all kinds of commercial construction projects. These projects may be located in a construction engineer's hometown, a neighboring state, or distant locations throughout the world. Wherever the work happens to be, construction engineers travel there.

Construction engineers play an important role in building and maintaining the world's critical infrastructure. *Infrastructure* refers to roads, highways, railways (aboveground and belowground), and airport traffic control towers. It also includes water supply and sewage treatment systems, telephone lines, cell phone towers, and electrical power lines and connections (known as the power grid), as well as the internet.

The world's bridges are another important part of the infrastructure. Construction engineers oversee the building of new bridges, but far more often they work on older bridges that are structurally unsound or just need some repairs. Construction engineer Andrew Giocondi worked on the Longfellow Bridge Rehabilitation Project, which is a historic bridge in Massachusetts that was built in 1908. "It has been one of the most challenging and unique projects I have ever worked on," says Giocondi. The bridge, which spans the Charles River, connects the cities of Boston and Cambridge and accommodates motor vehicle, bicycle, and pedestrian traffic, as well as the mass transit system. "Our team has been tasked with reconstructing the bridge to provide upgraded structural capacity while maintaining and restoring its historic nature,"[34] says Giocondi.

Foreign Service Construction Engineers

Construction engineers who work for the US Department of State (or State Department) are known as Foreign Service specialists. They may be stationed in the United States but spend most of their career assigned to missions elsewhere in the world. Foreign Service construction engineers are responsible for overseeing the US government's "multi-billion dollar portfolio of construction projects overseas,"[35] as the State Department website explains. This often includes US embassies and related facilities in other countries.

Foreign Service construction engineers have a wide variety of duties, including inspecting contractors' work to ensure it meets quality standards, ensuring that all materials used meet contract specifications, monitoring safety tasks, and managing security issues. Also part of a construction engineer's job description is administrative tasks, such as managing the site office, approving budgets, preparing inventories, hiring and managing local employees, ensuring property inventory control, and handling other site obligations, such as conducting tours for prominent visitors.

These sorts of tasks are very familiar to Stephanie Felton, a construction engineer who works for the State Department. Felton's primary job is to oversee and manage the construction companies that build US embassies, which are the official headquarters for US government representatives in foreign countries. One experience that stands out in her mind is when she was working in Haiti after the catastrophic 2010 earthquake. "The embassy there was one of the few buildings that was basically untouched,"[36] she says. Felton credits the contractors and the whole construction crew for building a structurally sound building that could stand up to an earthquake. With little damage to the embassy, she and her team were able to focus their efforts on assisting the cleanup and rebuilding operation in Haiti.

Education and Training

A career in construction engineering requires a bachelor's degree from a college or university whose engineering program is accredited by the Accreditation Board for Engineering Technology. Most construction engineers earn their degree in construction engineering, civil or structural engineering, electrical engineering, mechanical engineering, or architectural engineering. Aspiring construction engineers can expect a college curriculum that is heavy in math and science, including linear algebra, calculus, trig-onometry, chemistry, and geology. Other course work (depending on the school) may include construction surveying, construction technology and equipment, preconstruction management, engineering mechanics, and engineering ethics.

While they are attending college, aspiring construction engineers should take advantage of internship opportunities. Prospective employers value work experience nearly as much as a college degree, and young people with on-the-job experience are much more likely to be hired. Students enrolled in Purdue University's Construction Engineering and Management program are required to perform three twelve-week internships before graduating. The internships are paid and are normally completed during the summer, when students are on break from school. They gain valuable hands-on experience while working in their chosen field for employers throughout the United States or other countries. The Purdue website explains, "Students have worked as locally as their hometown and as far away as Norway!"[37]

Construction engineer Alexandra Sexton, who graduated from Purdue in May 2014, completed three internships while she was a student: one in her hometown of Chesterton, Indiana; one in downtown Chicago, Illinois; and one at the US Embassy in Oslo, Norway. All three internships were with the construction management firm the Walsh Group. Sexton gained invaluable work experience from each of the internships and also proved herself to be worthy of hiring. Upon college graduation, Sexton was hired by the Walsh Group to work full time in Oslo.

Skills and Personality

Construction engineers need a variety of skills and personality traits in order to be successful in their jobs. They must have strong math, science, and computer/technical skills and be highly proficient at problem solving. They must enjoy working outside because that is where they spend much of their time on the job. They need initiative, analytical ability, and the desire to learn in

(and adapt to) an environment that changes constantly. They also must have strong communication skills, including speaking, writing, and listening.

Also essential for construction engineers is the ability to get along well with others and build relationships with them. This includes their coworkers, clients, contract employees, and a host of others with whom they interact on a daily basis. "People may not know how people-oriented this career is," says construction engineer Maura Fox. "I learned the technical skills in college, but that is nothing compared to the persuasion, negotiation, leadership, and teamwork needed in order to be successful as an engineer."[38]

Working Conditions

Those who have chosen to work in construction engineering are aware that their working conditions are typically more rugged than some other engineering specialties. Construction engineers are in the office part of the time but spend far more time outdoors, at job sites. They also work a schedule that typically exceeds forty hours per week, and they are paid accordingly. "The downside to this though is you'll work for every extra dollar you make," says civil engineer Craig Bernard. "Hello 60–80 hour work weeks!"[39]

Spending so much of their time at job sites means that construction engineers pitch in and work hard—and invariably, they will perform duties that are physically taxing. The State Department is blunt about this in its May 2018 job posting for construction engineers. It notes that in the course of their jobs, construction engineers must spend prolonged periods of time standing, bending, and stretching. They are also likely to supervise contractors and tradespeople who work with building equipment, heavy machinery, and a variety of construction vehicles. "All of these tasks," says the job listing, "are at times performed at construction sites with ambient noise and other environmental factors that are typical for such sites."[40] In other words, construction engineering can be a tough, demanding job. It is probably not the best choice of careers for those who prefer a quiet inside environment and little physical effort.

Employers and Pay

Companies of all sizes employ construction engineers. The Bureau of Labor Statistics (BLS) offers detailed job information about the broader category of civil engineers and reports the following as the largest employers: the federal government, local governments, engineering service firms, state governments, and nonresidential building construction firms (in that order). Although Foreign Service construction engineers are typically happy with their jobs and highly recommend their employer, the State Department only hires a small number of construction engineers each year, so there are few jobs available.

Construction engineers are typically paid very well. For civil engineers (whose salaries are comparable to construction engineers), the BLS gives a salary range of $54,000 to more than $138,000 per year. Those whose jobs take them overseas often benefit from travel allowances and the ability to visit many fascinating parts of the world.

What Is the Future Job Outlook for Construction Engineers?

According to the BLS, civil engineers, a group that includes construction engineers, held 303,500 jobs in 2016. That number was projected to grow 11 percent by 2026, which means more than 32,200 civil engineering jobs will be created in the coming years. These jobs could be anywhere from New York City to Norway or Saudi Arabia, and qualified construction engineers who love to travel and want to work in distant places will likely be in high demand.

Find Out More

American Society of Civil Engineers (ASCE)
1801 Alexander Bell Dr.
Reston, VA 20191
website: www.asce.org

Founded in 1852, the ASCE is the United States' oldest engineering society. Its website offers education and career information, access to trade publications such as the *Civil Engineering* magazine, and a link to a construction engineering section.

EngineerGirl
National Academy of Engineering
500 Fifth St. NW, Room 1047
Washington, DC 20001
website: www.engineergirl.org

The EngineerGirl website was designed to bring public attention to the many opportunities in engineering for girls and women. The website is a valuable resource for all kinds of information about engineering careers, although its content does not include construction engineering.

Purdue University
Construction Engineering and Management
701 W. Stadium Ave.
West Lafayette, IN 47907
website: https://engineering.purdue.edu/CEM/academics /undergraduate

Purdue University offers a bachelor of science in construction engineering. The program's website contains a great deal of information for those who want to explore construction engineering careers, including an overview of the industry, plans of study, study abroad programs, and industry opportunities, as well as student success stories.

US Department of State
Office of Foreign Missions
2201 C St. NW, Room 2236
Washington, DC 20520
website: www.state.gov

The US Department of State advises the president and leads the country in foreign policy issues. Its Foreign Service professionals work throughout the United States, as well as more than 270 locations overseas. Its website's search engine links to numerous publications about Foreign Service construction engineer careers, including open positions.

Travel Nurse

A Few Facts

Number of Jobs
About 2.9 million*

Pay
About $48,690 to more than $100,000*

Educational Requirements
Minimum of associate's degree in nursing, bachelor's degree often preferred; licensure by the National Council of State Boards of Nursing

Personal Qualities
Critical-thinking skills, excellent communication skills, compassion, emotional stability, physical stamina, ability to adapt to ever-changing work environments

Work Settings
Hospitals, residential care facilities, urgent care clinics

Future Job Outlook
Projected 15 percent growth rate through 2026*

* Number is for all registered nurses, a group that includes travel nurses.

What Does a Travel Nurse Do?

A travel nurse is a registered nurse (RN) who travels around for work assignments, rather than working for one employer in the same place. Hospitals and other health care facilities contract with staffing agencies to provide experienced, qualified RNs for a certain period of time. Travel nurses (often called "travelers") can choose wherever they want to work, whether that is a small, rural village or a major metropolitan area. One example is Cherisse Dillard, who has been a travel nurse for more than a dozen years. She loves her job, including the travel, and has worked in Chicago, Illinois; Dallas and Houston in Texas; Pensacola, Florida; and San Francisco, California.

Travel nurses are typically contracted for thirteen weeks, but some assignments last longer. Once they finish an assignment, they may choose to accept a contract in another location and start a new job or take some time off in between. "By living life 13 weeks at a time," says travel nurse Candy Treft, "travel nurses get to choose if they are going to work back to back contracts, and if so, how much. That's the beauty of travel nursing!"[41]

Once they have been assigned to a health care facility, travel nurses become part of the staff. Their specific assignments depend on their specialty. Some, for instance, are pediatric nurses who work with children and teens, while others are oncology nurses who work with cancer patients. Geriatric nurses work with elderly patients, and labor and delivery nurses work with women before, during, and after they deliver their babies. Judy Vernon is a labor and delivery nurse who has worked as a travel nurse for many years. One assignment at a hospital in Montana was particularly memorable, as she explains: "I took care of a woman who was carrying twins and I was with her for several weeks until she gave birth. Since that time we've kept in touch, and I've had the good fortune of watching the twins grow."[42]

Some duties are basically the same no matter where the travel nurse works. Like all RNs, they observe patients and record their observations, assess patients' health conditions, and administer medicines and treatments as ordered by physicians. They help set up patient treatment plans and contribute information to existing plans. Other duties include consulting and collaborating with doctors and other health care professionals, operating and monitoring medical equipment, assisting with diagnostic tests, and analyzing the results of the tests. Also, nurses teach patients and their families how to manage illnesses or injuries, and they discuss at-home care after treatment.

On the Job

A day in the life of a travel nurse can vary tremendously from one location to another. Not all nurses are interested in such uncertainty and constant change, but for some it is part of the fun. "I like the challenge of adjusting to a new environment," says travel nurse Camille Prevost, "including working with new people and experiencing different cultures."[43]

When travel nurses start a new assignment, typically the first week or so is spent in orientation. This is when they learn about the facility, the level of care staff provides, and the patients who

Overcoming Loneliness

"One of my biggest fears before I started my travel nursing career was the fear of being alone. I was leaving everything and everyone I knew on an adventure to a place where I knew no one . . . a 13 week time constraint made it much more difficult [to meet people]; not to mention most of the people I was friends with were my co-workers, so I knew changing jobs every three months might put a damper on my social network. I was surprised to find that connecting with people on the road wasn't as difficult as I thought it was going to be."

—Crystal Gustafson, a travel nurse from Denver, Colorado

Crystal Gustafson, "Making Friends as a Travel Nurse," TravelNursing.org, August 19, 2016. www.travelnursing.org.

are treated there. "The first week will usually fly by as you attend orientation, and try to find your way around the facility, and back and forth to work," says Treft. "Simple tasks like [remembering] everyone's names [are] difficult for me for the first several weeks!"[44] During weeks two to four, Treft is focused on learning her routine and getting familiar with the facility's policies and procedures.

Things start to seem familiar to Treft after about the fourth week on the job. She has gotten to know the staff, she knows how to contact physicians and the pharmacy, and she has no problem finding the supplies she needs. By this time, she says, "I have found my confidence, can lose some of the 'newbie' jitters. . . . I finally have time to breathe, and can slow down and say hello to coworkers." Around week six, Treft is ready to do some exploring. She often goes for weekend jaunts to visit area tourist attractions. Sometimes she takes walking tours of a city or meets up with other travel nurses for dinner or drinks. "This is the best time to get out and enjoy being in a new city,"[45] she says.

Because she is a traveler at heart, during the last two or three weeks of her job assignment, Treft starts getting antsy to move on. "I have found that things can become monotonous for me,"[46] she says. When she is not working, she spends much of her time speaking with her recruiter and planning for the next assignment.

A travel nurse checks on her young patient. Travel nurses do the same work as other nurses except that they take temporary work assignments in hospitals and health clinics in different locations across the United States and around the world.

When that contract has ended and she gets to her next job, she starts the same process over again. To aspiring travel nurses, Treft has these words of advice: "If you're like me (and most travel nurses) and get bored easily, thrive on change, adventure and the unknown . . . maybe you should try living life 13 weeks at a time."[47]

Education and Training

A travel nurse's career begins with earning either an associate's degree in nursing or a bachelor of science in nursing (BSN). Both are accepted by most health care facilities, although a growing number prefer to contract only with BSNs. After graduation nurses must pass the National Council Licensure Examination, which is administered by the National Council of State Boards of Nursing. A passing grade makes them eligible to be licensed by the state in which they live. In addition to licensure, nurses can earn certification in specific areas, such as critical care, pediatrics, geriatrics, oncology, and ambulatory care, among others.

Once they are licensed, RNs can legally practice in all fifty US states and the District of Columbia. Before they become travel nurses, they should get a full-time nursing job and work for a few years. Employers are most likely to hire individuals who have at least a year of work experience.

Skills and Personality

Like all RNs, travel nurses must be good critical thinkers and excellent communicators. They must be compassionate and caring, be emotionally stable, and have the ability to remain calm in emergency situations. Physical stamina is essential because nurses are on their feet for most of their shift and must be able to move patients.

In addition to these qualities, travel nurses need to be flexible and able to adapt to all kinds of new and unfamiliar situations. "Being able to compromise and change in response to a situation is a key skill to being a good travel nurse," says an article on the Travel Nurse Across America blog. "To be flexible, you need to be capable of quickly changing the way you work to best fit your employer's needs."[48] And, of course, travel nurses must have a desire to travel and move around from place to place.

Working Conditions

The hours travel nurses work vary according to the facility. In general, they work three twelve-hour days, four ten-hour days, or five eight-hour days. This can be negotiated as part of a travel nurse's contract, along with which shifts will be worked (days or nights). If they accept an assignment and find that they don't like the job, they can take comfort in knowing that their tenure at the facility is short term. "I think one of the benefits of travel nursing is that we live, and survive, by the mentality, 'I can do anything for 13 weeks'—good, bad, or horrible,"[49] says Treft.

Even in the best work environments, travel nurses face challenges, especially during the first few weeks. "Starting over in a new unit is hard," says Courtni Sladek, a travel nurse who specializes in pediatrics. "You don't know anyone, how the unit runs, which person is going to share your off-the-wall sense of humor. If you didn't have social skills before, you'll definitely be acquiring them travel nursing." In Sladek's experience, most of her coworkers have been warm and welcoming toward her. "People are usually curious and want to know all about where you're from, where you've worked before, why you wanted to go into travel nursing,"[50] she says.

Employers and Pay

Travel nurses work for a variety of health care facilities, including hospitals, nursing homes, outpatient clinics, urgent care facilities, and physician offices—basically, any facility that employs nurses could potentially have a need for travel nurses. Just as travel nurses can choose which cities they want to work in, they have the freedom to select which health care facilities they prefer. Some like to work only in hospitals, whereas others prefer medical clinics or other settings.

The ability to earn a very good salary is an attractive benefit of travel nursing. According to the Bureau of Labor Statistics (BLS), RN earnings ranged from $48,690 to more than $100,000 per year as of May 2017. Depending on how many assignments per year they accept, travel nurses can earn even more than traditional nurses. Factors that influence their salaries include geographic location, specialty, and which shifts are worked. Along with their salaries, travel nurses receive extra compensation for housing, utilities, health insurance, and other benefits—like the ability to travel. "I don't look at traveling as a job," says a travel nurse from Mississippi named Jessica. "It's more like a mini-vacation . . . while working."[51]

What Is the Future Job Outlook for Travel Nurses?

In 2016 nurses in the United States held 2.9 million jobs. The BLS projects 15 percent growth through 2026, which equates to 438,100 new nursing jobs. As more and more health care decision-makers come to see the benefits of staffing with contract employees, the demand for travel nurses will likely soar.

Find Out More

American Traveler Staffing Professionals

1615 S. Federal Hwy., Suite 300
Boca Raton, FL 33432
website: www.americantraveler.com

American Traveler is a health care staffing agency. A great deal of information about travel nursing can be found on its website, including articles on salary, benefits, housing, and frequently asked questions, as well as job listings. A large collection of postings about travel nursing are available on the *Travel Nursing Blog*, which can be accessed through the website.

Gypsy Nurse

website: www.thegypsynurse.com

Gypsy Nurse is an active online community and information resource especially for travel nurses. The website offers a step-by-step travel nurse guide, interviews with travel nurses, and articles on numerous topics, including staffing agencies, jobs, destinations, housing, the good and bad of travel nursing, and much more.

Nurse Journal
website: https://nursejournal.org

Nurse Journal is an online social community for all kinds of nurses, including travel nurses. The website offers information on nursing degrees, financial aid, nursing specialties, and jobs. The pull-down menu at the top of the site links to a career section with many articles on travel nursing.

Travel Nursing
200 112th Ave. NE, Suite 310
Bellevue, WA 98004
website: www.travelnursing.org

Travel Nursing is an information resource for anyone who is interested in becoming a travel nurse. Its website offers information on the benefits of travel nursing, how to become a travel nurse, what to expect as a travel nurse, salary and compensation rates, and frequently asked questions about the travel nursing field.

Humanitarian Aid Worker

A Few Facts

Number of Jobs
About 162,200 in 2016*

Pay
About $26,600 to $87,440 in 2017

Educational Requirements
High school diploma to master's degree

Personal Qualities
Compassion, desire to serve others, problem-solving and communication skills, ability to adapt to changing scenarios, ability to work well with people of various cultures and beliefs

Work Settings
Countries all over the world, wherever people suffer from poverty, hunger, the effects of war, and natural disasters

Future Job Outlook
Projected 11 percent growth through 2026*

* Numbers are for organizations based in the United States.

What Does a Humanitarian Aid Worker Do?

There are thousands of humanitarian organizations throughout the world. As varied as these may be, they exist for a common reason: to relieve human suffering and save lives. Workers from these organizations assist people whose lives have been devastated by natural disasters, the effects of war, severe poverty and famine, and other types of crises.

Humanitarian aid worker is an umbrella term that refers to a huge variety of occupations that may include administrative aides, nurses, doctors, engineers, truck drivers, disaster relief workers, health education specialists, and a host of others. One humanitarian aid worker is Iffat Tahmid Fatema, who works for the humanitarian organization Oxfam International. She works in Bangladesh, a country in South Asia where Oxfam has set up refugee camps for Muslim people known as the Rohingya. Nearly three hundred thousand Rohingya escaped from life-threatening conditions in their native Myanmar and now live in the Oxfam camps. Fatema's job is to teach the refugees about health and hygiene in order to keep them healthy and prevent a disease outbreak. "We discuss the importance of cleanliness and personal hygiene, like washing your hands with soap after going to the toilet and before eating," says Fatema. "We work with volunteers from the Rohingya community, training them so they can teach other refugees and spread good hygiene messages far and wide."[52]

Some humanitarian aid workers specialize in helping people whose homes and communities have been struck by natural disasters, such as hurricanes, floods, and earthquakes. This is the specialty of the American Red Cross, which is part of the International Federation of Red Cross and Red Crescent Societies. When a disaster strikes, Red Cross relief workers begin coordinating plans for response efforts. "Workers take action to save lives, preserve property, and provide humanitarian care,"[53] says Elka Torpey, who is with the Bureau of Labor Statistics (BLS). According to Torpey, tasks performed by relief workers include evacuating affected areas, setting up shelters, repairing critical infrastructure, and delivering food, medicine, and other supplies to people affected by the disaster. Once people's immediate needs have been met and basic services have been restored, the recovery effort begins. Relief workers help rebuild communities and assist with economic recovery, which involves helping with housing, health, and social services needs. "People who work in disaster relief have a variety of jobs," says Torpey, "but they all have a common mission: ensuring that when disaster strikes, help follows."[54]

The Workday

The very nature of humanitarian work is doing whatever it takes to relieve human suffering and help people who need assistance. That can be a massive and unpredictable task—meaning that workers must be prepared for most anything and have no way of knowing what each day will bring. "There is no typical day!" says Ronald, who works for humanitarian group Mercy Corps in

Uganda, Africa. "I think this is a great thing, although it can be challenging having to be so flexible."[55]

Another humanitarian worker based in Uganda is Mary Maturu, who is with the CARE organization. Maturu is a midwife—a professional who is trained to assist pregnant women during labor and delivery and after their babies are born. Maturu educates girls and women on all kinds of issues, ranging from reproductive health care to gender-based violence. Each morning she arrives at a CARE women's center located in the Imvepi refugee settlement in northwestern Uganda. She organizes and maps out her day and then gets her consultation desk ready to meet with patients.

A big part of Maturu's day is spent traveling to refugee communities to see women there. Imvepi is a vast settlement that covers 58 square miles (150 sq. km), and many women have no way of getting to the women's center. During these home visits, Maturu discusses a variety of topics, one of which is family planning. She says this can be a sensitive topic to discuss because it involves sexual relations. Still, she says she emphasizes the importance of family planning to the women, "especially since we have seen quite a number of unwanted pregnancies in the settlement."[56]

In the afternoon Maturu heads back to the women's center, where she spends the rest of the day seeing as many women as possible. Many of them are pregnant and in need of advice about prenatal care and other matters. She tries to explain the importance of having their babies in a hospital, but most have never seen a doctor before and have no concept of hospitalization. At about 5:00 p.m., Maturu wraps up for the day and starts walking home. "The walk gives me time to reflect and revisit some of the things people have told me," she says. "Some of the stories are heartbreaking." Although there is always more to do in Imvepi than she can possibly manage, says Maturu, "I know that I am making a difference in the lives of hundreds of mothers here."[57]

Education and Training

Each humanitarian organization has its own educational requirements that differ depending on the specific occupation. At the American Red Cross, for instance, community health workers, social and human service assistants, and delivery service drivers are only required to have a high school diploma (or equivalent) and on-the-job training. Higher-level positions such as social and community service managers or fund-raisers need a bachelor's degree, and mental health counselors need a master's degree.

People who work for Oxfam, CARE, or other humanitarian organizations that are based in remote areas of the world nearly always have a bachelor's or master's degree. This is because competition is fierce among job applicants, as Suzanne Bearne, a journalist from the United Kingdom, explains: "The humanitarian and international relief field is tough to break into, with thousands of smart, ambitious and eager graduates trying to enter the profession."[58]

Work experience is as important as education for humanitarian workers. Young people who want a career in humanitarian aid should seriously consider volunteering with humanitarian organizations, which depend on volunteers to make their work possible. Internships are another way to get on-the-job experience. These are rarely paid positions, but aspiring humanitarian workers can earn college credits while gaining invaluable experience that could eventually help them get a permanent job.

Skills and Personality

Humanitarian aid work is not for everyone. People who choose it for their career must possess the ability and willingness to adapt to ever-changing, unpredictable circumstances. They also need good problem-solving skills and must be excellent communicators, adept at listening as well as speaking. They must work well in teams and be able to remain calm and levelheaded in challenging and difficult situations—which are part of the job for humanitarian aid workers. Another valuable and sometimes required skill is the ability to speak (or learn to speak) languages other than English.

Also essential for anyone who works in humanitarian aid is passion and a serious desire to help others. "You do it because you love it, and you believe in it," says Ted Murphy, who lectures on international relations and global studies at Northeastern University. "You need to be very dedicated to the cause of social justice. You have a passion for it as something you want to pursue in your career, and you want to make the world a better place."[59]

Working Conditions

A humanitarian aid worker's workplace can be in any part of the world where people are desperate for help. This might be in Bangladesh, Haiti, southern Syria, war-torn Yemen, or countries throughout Africa. The world is full of people in need, and wherever they are is also where humanitarian aid workers are.

In many of the countries where these workers are based, conditions are bleak, as veteran humanitarian worker Nick Macdonald explains: "The reality is that much relief and development work takes place in some of the more challenging locations in the world. . . . You may not have reliable access to the normal amenities of the western world like electricity, hot and cold running water, reliable heat and cooling, and the freedom of movement to explore at your leisure." Although humanitarian organizations do their best to remedy these situations to make their workers more comfortable, Macdonald says, "the conditions in some postings can be distinctly primitive."[60]

Employers and Pay

There are thousands of humanitarian aid organizations worldwide, and aspiring humanitarian aid workers could potentially work with any of them. According to the BLS, US-based humanitarian organizations employed 162,200 workers in 2016. These organizations include the American Red Cross, Feed the Children, Feeding

America, Samaritan's Purse, and United States Fund for UNICEF, among others. Some of the largest humanitarian aid employers outside the United States include the World Food Programme, with 14,000 employees; UNICEF, with more than 13,000 employees; CARE, with nearly 9,200 employees; and Oxfam, with 5,300 employees. The largest humanitarian organization in the world is the International Federation of Red Cross and Red Crescent Societies, which employs 450,000 people.

As for pay, humanitarian aid work is not a career that people choose in order to get rich. Yet experienced aid workers can make a good living, especially if they are based in countries where the cost of living is very low. Each organization has its own pay scale, and workers' wages tend to vary depending on their education, occupation, and experience level. The pay range for US-based humanitarian organizations, says the BLS, is from $26,600 to $87,440.

What Is the Future Job Outlook for Humanitarian Aid Workers?

The need for humanitarian aid workers is great—and is growing. According to the BLS, employment in US-based humanitarian organizations more than doubled between 1990 and 2017. The

BLS projects 11 percent growth through 2016, which amounts to 18,400 new jobs in the United States alone. That does not account for the jobs with thousands of other humanitarian organizations outside the United States, which experts predict will also have a growing need for staff in the years to come.

Find Out More

CARE
Chemin de Balexert 7–9
1219 Chatelaine (Geneva)
Switzerland
website: www.care.org

CARE's worldwide network of employees and volunteers works to save lives, defeat poverty, and achieve social justice. Its website offers a great deal of information about the organization's work, the people who have been helped, what its humanitarian workers do, how to become involved, and much more.

International Federation of Red Cross and Red Crescent Societies (IFRC)
PO Box 303
CH-1211 Geneva 19
Switzerland
website: www.ifrc.org

The IFRC, which is the world's largest humanitarian network, provides assistance to people throughout the world who suffer from all kinds of disasters and crises. Its website offers a wealth of information about the organization's work, the many challenges its workers address, and the difference they have made in the lives of people in distress.

Oxfam International
The Atrium
Chaka Road
Kilimani, Nairobi, Kenya
website: www.oxfam.org

Oxfam is an international confederation of organizations working together with partners and local communities in more than ninety countries. Its website offers publications about Oxfam's work, the countries it serves, and the issues it focuses on. The site links to its blog, which offers a large collection of articles about what its workers do in the course of their jobs.

Raptim Humanitarian Travel
Spoorlaan 308
5038 CC Tilburg
The Netherlands
website: www.raptim.org

Raptim is a travel agency that is specifically devoted to humanitarian organizations, helping them organize their travel needs throughout the world. Its website features publications about the work of humanitarian organizations, as well as a search engine that produces a variety of articles about humanitarian aid careers.

ESL Teacher

A Few Facts

Number of Jobs
About 250,000 worldwide

Pay
About $54,337 annual average salary (United States)

About $4,800 to $48,000 annual salary outside the United States

Educational Requirements
Bachelor's degree and appropriate teacher certifications

Personal Qualities
Adaptable and sensitive to cultural differences; excellent communication skills (listening, speaking, and writing); enthusiastic; genuinely care about students; patience

Work Settings
Public schools, private schools, and language academies in cities and towns throughout the world

Future Job Outlook
More than 100,000 new jobs each year

What Does an ESL Teacher Do?

Teachers of English as a second language (ESL) work in elementary schools, secondary schools, postsecondary schools, and academies throughout the world. Sometimes known as EFL (English as a foreign language) teachers, their job is to teach the English language to students of all ages, from young children to adults. For those who yearn to travel as part of their careers, being an ESL teacher might be the ideal job. "It is a good life if you love travelling and teaching,"[61] says Enna Morgan, an ESL teacher from the South American country of Guyana.

ESL teachers are tasked with helping students learn to read, write, and speak English. Students come from varied backgrounds, and teachers must pay attention to their particular strengths and challenges. "You get to know your students and . . . make adjustments to suit them,"[62] says ESL teacher Stephanie Gaertner. Along with classroom instruction, ESL teachers often spend time in the evenings and on weekends doing work that they cannot complete during the school day. This involves tasks such as preparing lesson plans and grading papers and tests. Also during this time, they may meet individually with students, parents, or other faculty.

Being able to travel is one of the things Gaertner appreciates most about her job. She became interested in exploring the world while spending time in Turkey, where she lived with a family and taught English to their children. That experience, she says, "opened my eyes to the absolute magic of traveling." After leaving Turkey, Gaertner had no interest in returning to her job in New York City. Instead, she was ready to explore the world. "That travel bug gets you!"[63] she says. Gaertner accepted a job in Thailand, where she taught English to students aged eight to thirteen.

A Typical Workday

Exactly what ESL teachers do in their jobs depends on the school, the customs of the country where they teach, and the ages of the students. For an ESL teacher named Judith, who teaches in Cambodia, a typical day at her job begins with a forty-five-minute ride to school in a tuk-tuk, which is a two-wheeled carriage pulled by a motorbike. When it is time for school to start, the children hurry eagerly to their classrooms. As many as eighty students occupy Judith's classroom, sitting in plastic chairs at long wooden desks. When they see her, they give her a warm greeting in unison: "Good morning Teacher."[64] They remain standing until their regular classroom teacher tells them they can sit down.

Judith begins her lessons with simple instructional commands designed to teach English while making learning fun for students. "Hands on head, hands on shoulders, knees and toes," she tells them. "We then all happily sing with actions 'Head, Shoulders, Knees and Toes,'" she says. All Judith's lessons are in English and involve a combination of singing, reading stories, games, practicing colors, and counting, as well as prayers. "They're so keen to hear and speak English," she says. "The school offers a quality education—and they're eager to learn, studying from 7:30 till the lunch break." During lunch other teachers often seek

Judith's help in improving their own English language skills. "I'm quizzed," she says. "How do you say jam? Autumn? Thursday? Thumb? Throw? The English language frustrates their tongues as Khmer [Cambodian language] does my own."[65]

After lunch, Judith returns to the classroom. One of her lessons is art, which is unfamiliar and intriguing to the students because it is not part of the traditional Cambodian curriculum. "Most of the children have never experienced the use of scissors, glue sticks, nor using textiles to create patterns and designs," says Judith. "They love colouring, cutting, pasting. I display samples of finished craft work, then encourage their own unique work, which we proudly display on the wall. I am touched by their active conversation about it in their own language."[66]

When school ends for the day, Judith hires a tuk-tuk to take her back home. "It is time for a cold drink of water from the fridge, and then preparation for an English class with teenagers at 5:30 this evening," she says. She rides her own motorbike to the class, where her teen students are eager for their English lessons. After that class ends, Judith rides her motorbike home. Although she often feels exhausted after a long day of teaching, she loves her job and finds it fulfilling. "Each of my five trips to teach English [in Cambodia] has delighted me," she says. "The faces, the smiles, the experience, the overwhelming feedback. It's seared in my memory with fullness and satisfaction."[67]

Education and Training

ESL teachers must earn a bachelor's degree from an accredited college or university. Most of these institutions offer dual programs that allow students to earn a degree and teacher certification at the same time. Students who already hold bachelor's degrees and later become interested in ESL teaching can enroll in specialized programs that lead to certification. Internships in an ESL setting are a great way for aspiring ESL teachers to get invaluable on-the-job experience.

You Have to Care

"You'll get students who don't want to be there, others who will never be able to speak mildly fluently, or be able to construct a full sentence, but you have to be able to show your caring side and help them. You have to want to help students improve their level and become better English learners. It's not always easy. When you have a terrible teenage class, or group of many adults, or a hyperactive bunch of seven-year olds, you'll wonder why . . . you became a teacher in the first place. It's those teachers who care and can turn a bad class around that survive."

—Barry O'Leary, an ESL teacher from the United Kingdom

Barry O'Leary, "Becoming an ESL Teacher: Day in the Life, and Pros and Cons," BazTefl, June 2018. www.baztefl.com.

One certification that is widely recognized and desired by a growing number of employers worldwide is CELTA. Originally, the acronym stood for "Certificate in English Language Teaching to Adults," but it now refers to "Certificate in Teaching English to Speakers of Other Languages." The CELTA course is offered in more than seventy countries. Students may attend classes full time, which takes four to five weeks; part-time for several months to a year; or online, which combines hands-on teaching practice with online self-study. Because the institutions that offer CELTA courses must adhere to strict standards, it is among the most prestigious of all ESL teaching certifications. "In fact," says Emily Monaco, a writer and translator from Paris, France, "you'll sometimes see job offers for English language teachers citing the CELTA specifically as a prerequisite to be hired."[68]

Skills and Personality

It takes a special kind of person to be a good and effective teacher, and that is especially true for those who teach English to non-English speakers. ESL teachers must genuinely care about their students and be patient and understanding with them, helping them feel positive about their progress rather than getting discouraged when they struggle. Teachers must also be sensitive and adaptable to cultural differences and have excellent communication skills, including listening, speaking, and writing. Although fluency in the language of the country where they're teaching is not usually required, ESL teachers should be able to communicate with their students. By the time their assignment has ended, they will likely be fluent in the language of the country in which they have been working.

Working Conditions

ESL teachers work in every conceivable type of place, from small public or private schools to large academies where adults learn English. Working conditions can drastically vary from place to place. In Cambodia, for instance, teachers must endure weather that can be very unpleasant. "The weather alternates between hot, humid and dusty or sluicing rain," Judith says of her experiences in that country. "Some nights it pours so heavily, that the main roads and lanes flood. The cities lack infrastructure to drain the water. Rain floods the dirt floors of my students' huts, soaking their mattresses."[69]

According to surveys of ESL teachers, some of the best working conditions for ESL teachers are in Japan, South Korea, and some parts of China. Salaries are generous, and benefits are excellent. In China, for instance, many schools pay for their ESL teachers' living accommodations and even foot the bill for teachers to fly home once a year and spend time with their families. Teachers also get a generous amount of time off, as one ESL teacher explains: "The best thing is the holidays. . . . The package we receive in China allows us to travel more than we could have dreamed of."[70]

Employers and Pay

ESL teachers work for a variety of employers throughout the world. In the United States they are typically hired by individual school districts. ESL teachers who want to work in other countries are often recruited and placed by agencies such as the In-

Young Cambodians meet their new English teacher, a woman who has traveled from another country to teach the students to read, write, and speak English. ESL teachers work in the United States, but many also find jobs in other countries.

ternational TEFL Academy, Reach to Teach, Maximo Nivel, UCE-TAM, or TEFL Heaven.

According to the jobs and recruiting website Glassdoor, the average annual salary for ESL teachers in the United States was $54,337 in 2018. Actual earnings often vary by state; the top-paying states are California, New York, Connecticut, West Virginia, and Illinois (in that order). For ESL teachers who aspire to work outside the United States, the top-paying countries are (in order) United Arab Emirates, Japan, Saudi Arabia, Kuwait, Oman, Taiwan, South Korea, and China.

What Is the Future Job Outlook for ESL Teachers?

The British Council, one of the largest providers of English language instruction in the world, states that there are 1.5 billion English language learners worldwide—and the number is growing. This has led to a high demand for skilled educators who can teach English. And according to the International TEFL Academy, each year more than one hundred thousand positions for

No Regrets

"Teaching English in China not only provides me with a salary and self-development prospects but also with the ability to travel, in the oldest civilization in the world, and to learn about the culture and custom of these beautiful people, whilst being paid to do so. The salary I earn is sufficient to travel in the holidays. . . . I have no regrets about having traveled here. I shall treasure the memories I have stored and keep in touch with the many friends I have been fortunate enough to make here."

—Julia, an ESL teacher from the United Kingdom

Quoted in Sara Roberts, "A Day in the Life of an ESL Teacher," LinkedIn, August 22, 2018. www.linkedin.com.

English teachers open worldwide—definitely a promising outlook for aspiring ESL teachers. "The number of English learners around the world is only expected to grow," says Kenneth Beare, an ESL teacher and trainer, who adds, "The demand for ESL and EFL teachers abroad has increased in recent years, with countries from India to Somalia calling for teachers to travel abroad and share their knowledge of English."[71]

Find Out More

ESLteacherEDU.org
website: www.eslteacheredu.org

ESLteacherEDU.org is an online resource for anyone working in the ESL teaching field or those who aspire to become ESL teachers. The site offers information about topics such as education, certification, and salaries, as well as a link to a blog that offers numerous informative publications.

Teacher.org
website: www.teacher.org

Teacher.org is an online resource for everyone from aspiring teachers to veteran teachers, including those whose specialty is

ESL. The website has a section titled ESL Teacher, which provides information about qualities ESL teachers need, educational requirements, job duties, job descriptions, and salaries by state.

TESOL International Association
1925 Ballenger Ave., Suite 550
Alexandria, VA 22314
website: www.tesol.org

The TESOL International Association is the largest professional organization for teachers of English as a second or foreign language. Its website offers many articles for aspiring ESL teachers, including a section on career development and an online career center.

ThoughtCo
1500 Broadway
New York, NY 10036
website: www.thoughtco.com

ThoughtCo is a reference site with expert-created educational content. Its search engine produces numerous articles of interest to aspiring ESL teachers, with topics such as how to become an ESL teacher, what the job is like, and job prospects (including outside the United States).

Logistician

A Few Facts

Number of Jobs
About 148,700 in 2016

Pay
About $44,820 to more than $120,000 as of May 2017

Educational Requirements
Bachelor's degree often required

Personal Qualities
Strong communication skills; organizational, problem-solving, and critical-thinking skills; dedication to customer service; ability to cope with stressful situations

Work Settings
Logistical departments of businesses, specialized logistics firms

Future Job Outlook
Projected 7 percent growth rate through 2026

What Does a Logistician Do?

The word *logistics* refers to all the processes and steps that are needed to get a product from its point of origin to wherever it needs to go, when it needs to be there—which can be a gargantuan task. The professionals in charge of logistics are called logisticians. They work in all kinds of industries, from retail, finance, and the military to global delivery and mailing services. These industries are located all over the world, which means that logisticians are as likely to work in other countries as they are in the United States.

Logistics is essential; the world's commerce could not survive without it. Yet as vital as logistics is, people don't think about it much (if at all) because it happens behind the scenes—they take the process for granted. When they use their phones to place an order on Amazon, for instance, they assume that the order will go through, their credit card will be charged, the merchandise will be boxed up, and the package will be shipped and delivered to their home, apartment, or business, as promised. "The majority of individuals, unless they are in the transportation or import/export business, have never considered how many miles the products they use on a daily basis have traveled," says Ashley Boroski, who is head of business development and strategy at Lilly & Associates International Transportation & Logistics. "Without logistics, there would be no products at your retail stores!"[72]

Logisticians have a great deal of responsibility, with tasks that vary based on the nature of their specific job and whom they work for. Some typical duties include managing a product's life cycle from design to delivery, developing good business relationships with customers and suppliers, and working closely with customers to understand their needs and how to meet those needs. These professionals also conduct regular reviews of logistical functions to identify areas that can be improved and come up with strategies to minimize cost and time required to transport goods and materials.

Logistics plays a major role in getting the world's products from point A to point B, but the field goes far beyond commerce. Logisticians also coordinate emergency response efforts in the wake of devastating natural disasters such as hurricanes, tornadoes, or earthquakes. In the immediate aftermath of a disaster, critical supplies such as food, water, and medicine must be quickly procured, transported, and distributed to affected populations. Skilled workers and volunteers must be dispatched to the site immediately. Making sure the necessary equipment, supplies, and people arrive quickly rests on the shoulders of logisticians—and it's a massive responsibility.

The Workday

Most logisticians would agree that their workdays are anything but typical. According to Jason Shuttleworth, who is director of US Sales at a global logistics company, every day is different, and every day brings new challenges. "One day you might be working with a modest local start-up, the next you may be coordinating a large-scale logistic strategy with a multinational firm," says

Shuttleworth. "It's no exaggeration to say that no two days are the same in the logistics industry, and the dynamic nature of the work makes for a challenging and fulfilling career."[73]

Logisticians often start their day early and are on the job by 7:00 or 8:00 a.m. They check email to see whether there are any critical customer or supplier issues that must be addressed immediately. If so, the morning may be spent resolving those issues over the phone, via email, or in person. Other morning tasks could include meetings with staff or working out logistical plans or financial analyses on the computer. The afternoon may find a logistician visiting local customers. Then it's back to home base to review and approve documents and coordinate an important delivery for the next day. At around 6:00 p.m., just as it's time to go home, an important call sometimes comes through. "You're trying to clear your desk, but, all of a sudden, the phone rings," says logistics management professional Ben Benjabutr. "You have an 'Oh No' moment." The logistician quickly calls people together for an impromptu meeting to solve the urgent issue and afterward can finally leave for the day—but people who work in logistics often have trouble leaving the job responsibilities back at the office. "You talk in your sleep," says Benjabutr. "Better Cheaper Faster, Better Cheaper Faster, Better Cheaper Faster."[74]

Education and Training

Although some logisticians have associate's degrees, employers typically expect them to have a bachelor's degree. This was revealed in 2016 when Rasmussen College analyzed fifty thousand logistics job postings and found that 76 percent of employers preferred candidates with a bachelor's degree. Many logisticians get their degree in business, supply chain management, logistics, process engineering, or industrial engineering. Aspiring logisticians should look into internship opportunities while in college, since on-the-job experience is very important to potential employers. After working in a job for a few years, logisticians who are interested in being promoted to top management positions often get graduate degrees, such as a master of business administration.

Skills and Personality

People who have been successful at logistics careers are those who are confident, self-assured, and exceptional thinkers. They have strong communication skills, including listening as well as speaking. They must be extremely organized and excellent at solving all kinds of problems—just part of the job for people in logistics. Logisticians need strong numerical and analytical skills in order to analyze and interpret data, as well as technical skills and a familiarity with different types of computer software. And because logisticians constantly interact with customers, suppliers, and coworkers, they must have very strong interpersonal and relationship-building skills. "We interact with a variety of people from a variety of cultures and industries and building rapport is key to being successful,"[75] says Terri Danz, director of Dakini International Logistics.

Working Conditions

People in the field of logistics work in all sorts of settings, from manufacturing plants to product distribution centers and everything in between. "From an office to a factory floor or a delivery center, your daily workplace could take any form,"[76] says Shuttle-worth. Wherever logisticians are based, it is common for them to travel around to visit clients, which could take them across town or across the world. For those who long to travel, this aspect of a logistics career is very attractive. Shuttleworth writes, "Working with people from all over the world can open your eyes to new possibilities and ideas."[77]

One particularly challenging part of a logistician's job is the stress involved. Those who work in the industry usually agree that their jobs can be very stressful and sometimes a bit overwhelming. "A logistician's work is dauntingly complex," says Mitch MacDon-ald, group editorial director of AGiLE Business Media. "There's the relentless pressure to cut costs, which means doing more with less. And more than likely, you'll be expected to accomplish that without sacrificing customer service—in fact, you may even be expected to see that service improves. It's a profession that requires a highly advanced management skill set."[78]

Employers and Pay

According to the Bureau of Labor Statistics (BLS), the largest employers of logisticians in 2016 were manufacturing industries, followed by the federal government. Other large employers of lo-gisticians included professional, scientific, and technical service firms; businesses that manage companies and enterprises; and wholesale trade operations (in that order). "Logisticians work in almost every industry,"[79] says the BLS.

Salaries for logisticians are based on many factors, such as the size of the company for which they work and their level of responsibility. The BLS says that as of May 2017, logisticians in the United States earned from $44,820 to more than $120,000 per year. The highest-paying employers were the federal govern-ment, where the average annual salary was $84,200; profes-sional, scientific, and technical services ($74,900); manufacturing ($74,580); management of companies and enterprises ($74,190); and wholesale trade operations ($65,460).

An Unglamorous Profession

"It has often been said that no one goes into this profession for the glory. Logistics in particular can be thankless. If you keep things running smoothly and consistently, it will likely go unnoticed. The highest compliment you'll receive most days is that your phone didn't ring because all of your company's products and assets were where they were supposed to be when they were supposed to be there. You don't get a lot of public praise for making those things happen each and every day. Most people, in fact, have no idea that without logisticians, commerce would come to a halt."

—Mitch MacDonald, group editorial director of AGiLE Business Media

Mitch MacDonald, "The Thankless Life of a Logistician," *Supply Chain Quarterly*, October 2, 2015. www.supplychainquarterly.com.

What Is the Future Job Outlook for Logisticians?

The BLS reports that the total number of logistician jobs in 2016 was 148,700, and the agency's projection for the future is 7 percent growth by 2026. That equals 10,300 new logistician jobs being created in the coming years. Logistics management professional Chuck Edwards wants young people to know about careers in logistics because the field is often overlooked. "I think the challenge we have is the same for lots of manufacturing companies," says Edwards. "How do you communicate to college kids that this stuff is cool?" Edwards and other logistics professionals are working to build awareness among young people. "The more we can get face-to-face with kids, the better we can explain where the real excitement, and the future growth, is,"[80] he says.

Find Out More

Council of Supply Chain Management Professionals (CSCMP)
333 E. Butterfield Rd., Suite 140
Lombard, IL 60148
website: https://cscmp.org

The CSCMP supports its members by providing networking, career development, and educational opportunities. Its website features news releases, newsletters, social media links, and a search engine that produces a number of publications about logistics education and careers.

Institute for Supply Management (ISM)
309 W. Elliot Rd., Suite 113
Tempe, AZ 85284
website: www.instituteforsupplymanagement.org

The ISM is the oldest and largest supply management association in the world. Its website offers a special career center section and links to a number of publications about the field of supply chain management and logistics.

Supply Chain Quarterly
Tower Square, Number 4
500 E. Washington St.
North Attleboro, MA 02760
website: www.supplychainquarterly.com

Supply Chain Quarterly is a publication for supply chain professionals, including logisticians. The website's search engine produces a large variety of articles of interest to anyone considering a career in logistics.

Source Notes

Careers on the Move

1. Quoted in Elka Torpey, "Career Planning for High Schoolers," Bureau of Labor Statistics, January 2015. www.bls.gov.
2. Jacqueline Dautaj, "Career Planning for Teens," Love to Know. https://teens.lovetoknow.com.
3. Quoted in Emily Morgan, "Teens of the Month: Kardohely, Tegtmeier Segue Personal Interests into Career Paths," *Wooster (OH) Daily Record*, November 27, 2017. www.the -daily-record.com.
4. Quoted in Brian Tibbs, "An Inside Look at Careers in Hospitality," *DuPage at Work* (blog), June 8, 2016. www.worknet dupage.org.
5. Ashley Stahl, "7 Ideal Jobs for People Who Love to Travel," *Forbes*, April 24, 2017. www.forbes.com.

Hospitality Manager

6. Quoted in Andy Orin, "Career Spotlight: What I Do as a Hotel Manager," Life Hacker, January 20, 2015. https://lifehacker .com.
7. Quoted in Jemma Smith, "6 Reasons to Get into Hotel Management," Prospects, October 2018. www.prospects.ac.uk.
8. Quoted in Caitlin Raux, "How a People-Person with a Travel Bug Made a Career in Hospitality," Institute for Culinary Education, March 1, 2017. www.ice.edu.
9. Quoted in Raux, "How a People-Person with a Travel Bug Made a Career in Hospitality."
10. Quoted in Raux, "How a People-Person with a Travel Bug Made a Career in Hospitality."
11. Quoted in Elly Earls, "10 Things Every Hotelier Should Know," The Caterer, July 13, 2016. www.thecaterer.com.
12. Quoted in Tibbs, "An Inside Look at Careers in Hospitality."
13. Quoted in Orin, "Career Spotlight."

14. Quoted in Orin, "Career Spotlight."
15. Quoted in Raux, "How a People-Person with a Travel Bug Made a Career in Hospitality."

Event Planner

16. Kennedy, "What Kinds of Events Do Event Planners Produce?," 2018. http://kennedycreativeevents.com.
17. Quoted in Stacey Lastoe, "I'm an Event Manager and I Love Working with People," The Muse, 2018. www.themuse.com.
18. Quoted in Lastoe, "I'm an Event Manager and I Love Working with People."
19. Quoted in Lastoe, "I'm an Event Manager and I Love Working with People."
20. Quoted in The Muse editor, "How to Break Into Event Planning," 2018. www.themuse.com.
21. Lindsay Martin-Bilbrey, "5 Reasons We Love Being Event Planners," Pathable, August 17, 2017. https://pathable.com.
22. Quoted in *U.S. News & World Report*, "Meeting, Convention and Event Planner—Career Rankings, Salary, Reviews, and Advice," 2017. https://money.usnews.com.
23. Holly Barker, "The Rollercoaster Effect of Event Planning," *Event Manager Blog*, May 5, 2016. www.eventmanagerblog.com.
24. Barker, "The Rollercoaster Effect of Event Planning."
25. Bureau of Labor Statistics, "Meeting, Convention, and Event Planners," April 24, 2018. www.bls.gov.

Flight Attendant

26. Quoted in Rachel Gillett, "During Plane Emergency, Flight Attendants Know Exactly What to Do," Business Insider, April 20, 2018. www.businessinsider.com.
27. Quoted in Char Adams, "Southwest Passengers Describe How 'Hero' Flight Crew Jumped 'Into Action' After Engine Explosion," *People*, April 20, 2018. https://people.com.
28. Quoted in Rachel Gillett, "A Day in the Life of a United Airlines Flight Attendant," Business Insider, August 13, 2018. www.businessinsider.com.
29. Quoted in Gillett, "A Day in the Life of a United Airlines Flight Attendant."

30. Quoted in Workopolis, "What's It Like Working as a Flight Attendant?," February 12, 2018. https://careers.workopolis.com.

31. Quoted in Workopolis, "What's It Like Working as a Flight Attendant?"

32. Carrie A. Trey, "How to Become a Flight Attendant," Points Guy, September 5, 2017. https://thepointsguy.com.

33. Daphni Edwards, "Everything You Wanna Know About Being a Flight Attendant," Yung Jetlag, October 26, 2017. www.yungjetlag.com.

Construction Engineer

34. Quoted in *Constructive Thinking* (blog), Skanska USA, "Celebrating National Engineers Week," February 23, 2017. http://blog.usa.skanska.com.

35. US Department of State, "Construction Engineer—Careers," 2018. https://careers.state.gov.

36. Quoted in US Department of State, "Becoming a Foreign Service Officer," 2017. https://careers.state.gov.

37. Purdue University, "What Is Construction Engineering and Management?," 2018. https://engineering.purdue.edu.

38. Quoted in Skanska USA, "Celebrating National Engineers Week."

39. Craig Bernard, comment on Quora, "What Is the Difference Between a Construction Engineer and a Civil Engineer?," June 13, 2017. www.quora.com.

40. US Department of State, "Construction Engineer—Careers."

Travel Nurse

41. Candy Treft, "Life: 13 Weeks at a Time—as a Travel Nurse," The Gypsy Nurse, March 17, 2017. www.thegypsynurse.com.

42. Quoted in Andrya Feinberg, "5 Things Travel Nurses Love About Their Profession," Onward Healthcare. www.onwardhealthcare.com.

43. Quoted in Michelle Wojciechowski, "Here, There, and Everywhere: The Life of a Travel Nurse," *Daily Nurse*, July 18, 2017. https://dailynurse.com.

44. Treft, "Life."

45. Treft, "Life."
46. Treft, "Life."
47. Treft, "Life."
48. Travel Nurse Across America, "Must-Have Skills to Be a Travel Nurse," October 5, 2016. www.nurse.tv.
49. Treft, "Life."
50. Courtni Sladek, "The First Month in the Life of a Travel Nurse," Travel Nursing, July 10, 2017. www.travelnursing.org.
51. Quoted in Aya Healthcare, "Meet Jessica: Aya Healthcare Travel Nurse Stories & Reviews," 2018. www.ayahealthcare.com.

Humanitarian Aid Worker
52. Iffat Tahmid Fatema, "Five Things I've Learned Being a Humanitarian Aid Worker," *Conflict & Emergencies* (blog), Oxfam International, August 18, 2018. https://blogs.oxfam.org.
53. Elka Torpey, "Careers in Disaster Relief," Bureau of Labor Statistics, July 2018. www.bls.gov.
54. Torpey, "Careers in Disaster Relief."
55. Quoted in Mercy Corps, "World Humanitarian Day: Celebrating Our Dedicated Team," August 12, 2017. www.mercycorps.org.
56. Mary Maturu, "A Day in the Life: A Midwife in a Refugee Camp in Uganda," CARE, August 18, 2017. https://care.ca.
57. Maturu, "A Day in the Life."
58. Suzanne Bearne, "How to Find a Career in Humanitarian and International Relief Work," *Guardian* (Manchester), September 21, 2016. www.theguardian.com.
59. Quoted in Tamar Shulsinger, "Building a Humanitarian Career: How to Find a Job You Love," Northeastern University, October 31, 2017. www.northeastern.edu.
60. Nick Macdonald, "Why You Might Want to Work in Relief and Development (and Why You Might Not)," *Humanitarian Jobs* (blog), January 15, 2016. https://humanitarianjobs.wordpress.com.

ESL Teacher
61. Enna Morgan, comment on Quora, "How Much Demand Is There for ESL Teachers, and How Competitive Is the ESL Job Market?," March 24, 2017. www.quora.com.

62. Quoted in TEFL Heaven, "Q&A Interview with Stephanie Gaertner for TEFL Heaven Thailand," May 22, 2018. www .teflheaven.com.

63. Quoted in TEFL Heaven, "Q&A Interview with Stephanie Gaertner for TEFL Heaven Thailand."

64. Judith, "My Story: A Day in the Life Teaching English in Cambodia," Go. Serve. Love., June 8, 2018. https://goservelove .net.

65. Judith, "My Story."

66. Judith, "My Story."

67. Judith, "My Story."

68. Emily Monaco, "What's the Difference Between CELTA and TEFL?," Go Overseas, April 2018. www.gooverseas.com.

69. Judith, "My Story."

70. Quoted in Ciara Kenny, "Teaching in Britain: Long Hours, High Stress, 'Immense Pressure,'" *Irish Times* (Dublin), February 6, 2017. www.irishtimes.com.

71. Kenneth Beare, "How Many People Learn English?," Thought-Co, October 8, 2018. www.thoughtco.com.

Logistician

72. Quoted in Will Erstad, "What Is Logistics? Examining This Overlooked Industry," Rasmussen College, August 31, 2015. www.rasmussen.edu.

73. Jason Shuttleworth, "Five Reasons to Pursue a Career in Logistics," *Forbes*, April 27, 2018. www.forbes.com.

74. Ben Benjabutr, "What Does a Supply Chain Manager Do? A Day in the Life," SupplyChainOpz, January 2016. www .supplychainopz.com.

75. Quoted in Erstad, "What Is Logistics?"

76. Shuttleworth, "Five Reasons to Pursue a Career in Logistics."

77. Shuttleworth, "Five Reasons to Pursue a Career in Logistics."

78. Mitch MacDonald, "The Thankless Life of a Logistician," *Supply Chain Quarterly*, October 2, 2015. www.supplychain quarterly.com.

79. Bureau of Labor Statistics, "Logisticians," April 13, 2018. www.bls.gov.

80. Quoted in Anne Fisher, "Wanted: 1.4 Million New Supply Chain Workers by 2018," *Fortune*, May 1, 2014. http://fortune.com.

Interview with an ESL Teacher

Cara Canning, a teacher from Massachusetts, is currently working in Madrid, Spain. She teaches at a *concertado*, which is Spanish for "charter school." This is her third year as an ESL teacher. She answered questions about her career by email.

Q: What was your career path to where you are now?

A: Well, in college I majored in Geological Sciences and Spanish Studies, so I wasn't exactly heading toward education. After studying abroad in Granada, Spain, my junior year, I desperately wanted to return to Spain and continue exploring, and teaching English was one way to get there. I figured since I love kids and didn't want to pursue a career in geology at the moment, I had nothing to lose. It was the best decision I have ever made.

Q: Why did you become an ESL teacher?

A: My ESL teaching days began as a means to an end. I started teaching in order to live in Spain and travel throughout Europe. I was lucky enough to fall in love with teaching and find a future career that I wanted to pursue. I am currently pursuing my ESL teaching license in my home state of Massachusetts.

Q: Could you describe your typical workday?

A: I work from 9:00 a.m. until 5:00 p.m., with a half-hour break from 10:30–11:00 a.m. for *recreo* (recess) and a two-hour break from 12:30–2:30 p.m. for lunch. This schedule is quite standard for most ESL teachers, including the long break. During the day, I teach English language, natural sciences, and arts, all in English. I am not, however, alone in the classroom. I am considered the English language *auxiliar*, which is "assistant" in English. I teach while the main English teacher, who is Spanish, observes, assists, evaluates, and co-teaches. This year, I am teaching first, second, and third grades of primary school. During the previous two years, I taught five-year-olds in *infantil* (kindergarten) through sixth grade of primary school.

Q: What do you like most about your job?

A: I like being able to work with young people every day. More importantly, I love being a role model for them. Some students need more guidance and support than others, of course, but it's gratifying to know that regardless of what they have going on at home, I did all I could to help them be better than they were yesterday with the time we had together.

Q: What do you like least about your job?

A: Although I'm in charge of the class while I am teaching, I wish that I had a classroom to call my own to create more meaningful relationships with the young people I teach. The students, especially the younger ones, mostly adore the English auxiliares, but having the power to make more important decisions regarding their education and wellbeing is something I would like. In addition, each English auxiliar program limits the number of years an auxiliar can teach—which means at some point we have to leave. If not for that limitation, many of us would stay in our positions forever.

Q: What personal qualities do you find most valuable for this type of work?

A: Above all, patience and flexibility. Being in an adopted country means you must adapt to new surroundings in your social and work environments, and this can be very challenging. You'll be expected to adjust to the customs of the country you're in. And not only that, you must cope with factors out of your control, such as how others perceive you, whether they appreciate your work, and what their expectations are for teaching. You simply must be very patient, flexible, and open-minded to be an ESL teacher— and of course, you must love children.

Q: Have you been able to do a lot of traveling while you've lived in Spain?

A: Fortunately, I have been lucky enough to visit many countries in Europe during my three years here. In my first year of teaching I had Fridays off, and spent that time traveling to many European cities. Spain, because of its extensive Catholic tradition, requires its schools to take multiple weeks off for Christmas during winter and another week off for Easter during *Semana Santa* (Holy Week) in March or April. Flights within Europe are relatively cheap, and during these long weekends and holidays I have traveled to numerous countries: England, Portugal, Morocco, Belgium, the Netherlands, Germany, Italy, Austria, Hungary, the Czech Republic, Poland, Sweden, Denmark, Switzerland, and of course, I have explored all over Spain.

Q: What advice do you have for students who might be interested in this career?

A: If you are at all interested in ESL teaching, regardless of the country, I would definitely recommend that you pursue it. This experience has given me a purpose in my career when I lacked one and has allowed me to explore the world at the same time. Personally, I don't think it was a hard decision for me to move across the world—I had few responsibilities, had my whole life ahead of me, and realized I had only seen a small part of the world. If this sounds like you, pack your bags and take off for wherever you dream of living. You have nothing to lose.

Other Careers If You Like to Travel

Airline pilot

Archaeologist

Athletic recruiter

Auditor

Au pair/nanny

Computer support specialist

Cruise ship or yacht worker

Customer-service
representative

Freelance designer

Hotel concierge

Network/computer systems
administrator

Peace Corps volunteer

Professional chef

Publicist

Restaurant server or bartender

Retail buyer

Sales representative

Sports or fitness instructor

Tour guide

Translator

Travel agent

Travel photographer

Travel writer/blogger

Truck driver

Editor's note: The online *Occupational Outlook Handbook* of the US Department of Labor's Bureau of Labor Statistics is an excellent source of information on jobs in hundreds of career fields, including many of those listed here. The *Occupational Outlook Handbook* may be accessed online at www.bls.gov/ooh.

Index

Note: Boldface page numbers indicate illustrations.